Introduction

First and foremost thank you to all of the wise sensei's that have given the words of wisdom over the years, without who this would not have been possible.

The inspiration for this book came from a thought that knowledge is there to be shared. This a small portion of quotes and training tips that I have heard and learnt along the years and also my personal thoughts and opinions on these.

The wise sensei is the person who I originally heard these quotes from rather than the person who originally said them. Some of the holistic quotes are credited to those who originally said them.

I hope you enjoy the quotes and if you have any comments, questions or feedback please get in touch.

Contents

Chapter 1   **Sparring tips & Tricks**

Chapter 2   **Kata Performance tips**

Chapter 3   **Habit & Mindset**

Chapter 4   **Determination & Spirit**

Chapter 1

Sparring tips and tricks

*A wise Sensei once said
In a dojo not so far away*

"Stop trying to hammer square pegs into round holes"

-Jason Smith

If we break this down you can go two ways:
one being the negative and saying ok I'm rubbish at this so I will give up and do something else.

Second being the positive way. Say to yourself fair enough it may not be my strength, but I will work other areas that are my round pegs and make them stronger. At the same time I will work on my weaknesses to make them as strong as I can for my limitations.

Just an example: you may have great kicks but not so great strikes. So do you ignore the fact that your strikes are not strong and solely focus on your kicks, or do you develop your kicks further while finding ways to work with your limitations and improve your strikes?

I know what I would choose. Now remember when you are next in the dojo ask yourself what am I good at. Keep these things at the forefront of your mind. This positive mindset will help you to learn and grow. If we stress on the square pegs and keep trying to force them into the round holes we will not grow.

So be positive, train hard and be awesome.

*A wise Sensei once said
in a dojo not so far away*

"A building is as strong as its foundations"

Let's apply this to karate. Your body is the building and your legs are the foundations.

If you have poor stances do you think you will be able to generate power effectively?

So remember this next time you are in a dojo and Sensei shouts "bend your knees" or "these things are called knees and they bend".

Train hard and smile.

*A wise Sensei once said
in a dojo not so far away*

"Move towards what you know and away from what you don't know"

Let's look deeper into this for a second and apply this to sparring or a combat situation.

You want to move towards the striking hand side to either evade your opponent or gain a better position. You know what that striking hand is doing (aiming to hit you) where as the intentions of other hand are unknown to you.

So when you next spar in the dojo bare this principle in mind.

It might just help in avoiding a strike or kick.

*A wise Sensei once said
in a dojo not so far away*

"How do you hide a mountain with a grain of sand? Throw it in their eyes."

-Author Unknown

Let's apply this to sparring. Show your opponent what you want them to see.

So if you are throwing a kick disguise it with your hands.

Throw some punches to distract their attention and draw their guard away from the area that you wish to kick.

Then kick them in the gap so that they are less likely to defend it and take the advantage.

In other words punch like a kicker and kick like a puncher. So have a higher stance when punching to help trick their mind into thinking you favour kicking and a lower stance when kicking to give the impression of favouring punches.

*A wise Sensei once said
in a dojo not so far away*

"Closest weapon, closest target."

This one is quite self explanatory. If my fist is close to my opponents face then it would be a wasted opportunity if I don't hit them with it.

In all seriousness the closest weapon will be the fastest in most encounters,
so even if it is used to disrupt or even stop their forward momentum you can use the power shot to finish them off.

*A wise Sensei once said
in a dojo not so far away*

"I'm sure I could outrun Usain Bolt Providing I punched him in the head before we set off."

-Iain Abernethy

Although this is a funny quote and it was said by very a well known and
knowledgeable Sensei it makes sense. This is for two reasons, on the surface the brain controls the bodies movements so if you crash the computer can they function?

In one word no.

On a second note look at it this way, use your strengths to cause your opponent a disadvantage. So if you can strike hard use these in the right places.
If you are faster than your opponent then great use that to get either around them to create angles etc or to hit them before they hit you.

The long and short of it guys use your strengths to exploit the opponents
weaknesses both inside and outside of the dojo.

Chapter 2

Kata Performance Tips

*A wise Sensei once said
in a dojo not so far away*

"Do you want to know the secret to speed? Slow your technique down, this will make you faster"

-Kris Wilder

Now reading this you are thinking this Sensei has lost his or her marbles. How can going slower make me faster?

Let's turn this on its head.
If you slow down this allows you to break the move down into individual sections. You can then look at each section and take out the unnecessary bits i.e trim the fat and then speed it back up.
This will make your technique faster.

Just an example, let's look at a stomach level punch. So if you wish to punch faster slow it down and look at your technique in a mirror.

Check your elbows that they are not flaring, check that your shoulder is relaxed and also relax and tense at the end of the strike just before the point of impact. This will allow you to punch faster.

*A wise Sensei once said
in a dojo not so far away*

"All kata use the so called postures (kamae). In fact, there are many kinds of postures and many kinds of kata. While learning these postures should not be totally ignored, we must be careful not to overlook that they are just forms or templates of sort; it is the function of their application which needs to be mastered."

-Choki Motobu

This can be applied to any kata.

It's the principles of movement that the postures and stances teach us is of   importance. So for example in a self defence situation you wouldn't say to your attacker hold on while I form a good nikoashi dachi (cat stance).

Instead you would use the principle of shifting your weight and using the lead leg to attack or just to avoid the opponent.

So when you next look at a movement in kata try to look at the principles it is teaching us not just the movement itself.

*A wise Sensei once said
In a dojo not so far away*

"Who thinks breathing is important?"

- A.S Chodha

On the surface this looks like pure sarcasm. Yes sensei's do sometimes have a twisted sense of humour, but on this occasion it's not a joke.
Breathing is important for survival, but it also affects many other things.
If we are in a panic state we tend to breathe faster or hyperventilate.

When we are calmer we breathe slower and more naturally.
By timing breathing correctly you can increase the strength of your technique or even help your body to relax and make your techniques faster.

So when you are next in the dojo, watch how you breathe.
Be conscious of your breathing and if you are unsure about how or when to breathe ask your Sensei.

*A wise Sensei once said
in a dojo not so far away*

***"Karate is supposed to be uncomfortable.
When it becomes comfortable then adjust to make it uncomfortable again."***

-Sam Karagiannidis

This quote broken down makes more sense. When you first hear it you go huh? Did Sensei tell us to injure ourselves? No that is not the case.
What the quote says is that push your limits and move out of your comfort zone, as this is how we grow.

Let's take sumo stance (Shiko dachi) as an example. If we push down in stance and hold for say 10 seconds, it hurts. If you repeat this 10 second technique for a period, you will find your body will adapt and you will find it easier to hold   position.

You then extend that period and it becomes hard again. You repeat this process until you can hold for the desired period.

So guys the choice is yours. Will you choose comfort or will you choose to grow?

A wise Sensei once said in dojo not so far away

"The secret to snap in your movements? Prep, step and deliver."

-Kirsty Mallinder

This is a concept that will allow you to develop explosive power and strength in your techniques. It involves saving the hip twist till the end of the movement to give maximum power for your technique.

An example of where we can use this is stepping forwards and back in ko Kutso dachi stance.

So breaking it down prepare your hands/feet as necessary for the technique, step through, but do not set the stance. Finally snap the hips and lock the stance and finish.

*A wise Sensei once said
in a dojo not so far away*

"It's done like this in the kata, but it's different in self defence."

When we practice kata we can add intent to moves that would be dangerous to do with a partner.

A good example would be the neck crank at the end of Saifa. You can practice this full power in the kata, but cannot with a partner. The same way we have to adapt moves to do them safely with a partner.

The second reason is pure aesthetics. Certain moves are done in a way to look good, as if you did them in a 'dirty' fashion it would make the kata look less polished and messy.

Chapter 3

Habit & Mindset

*A wise Sensei once said
in a dojo not so far away*

"You can only fight the way you practice"

-Miyamoto Musashi

As humans we are creatures of habit.
If we practice with loose fists and bent wrists, guess what happens when we have to use those techniques in a high pressure and adrenaline filled environment?
If we only ever practice the shortcuts then that's all you will ever know.
So when you are next in the dojo push yourself as far as you can (without risking injury).

*A wise sensei once said
in a dojo not so far away*

"Find a partner someone who you don't usually work with."

This is an important factor guys. There is a famous quote from Miyamoto Musashi the swordsman
"If you only ever study one planet how can you understand the universe?"

What he means by this is that if you only ever fight one person or work drills with one person you only ever gain understanding of that one person and how they fight. If you try various opponents you will gain a greater understanding of how different people of shapes and sizes fight.

This is a great reason to also enter tournaments. Test your skills against others of similar age, but different body types and also fighting styles.

Now next time you get told to pair up, go wild and pick someone different.

*A wise Sensei once said
in a dojo not so far away*

"*Practice makes permanent.*"

- Author Unknown

Habits are easily formed, but are very hard to change/break.
As an example this is the reason why we practice basics every class. By repeating techniques often, your muscles remember the movements involved and hence they become easier to perform.

Just another example by the time you achieve your black belt you will have thrown hundreds of thousands of head level punches and guess what ?
Even at that level you will still find ways of improving your technique.
Either by relaxing more or keeping your elbows in etc.

So remember guys when you practice in the dojo put in 100% as this is what your muscles will remember and it will become permanent.

*A wise Sensei once said
in a dojo not so far away*

"You either win or learn, there is no loosing."

-Author Unknown

This is one of my personal favourites, let's apply this to tournaments. Most people think if they don't win a medal they have failed.
This could not be further from the truth. By having the courage to enter in the first place is a victory and on top of that the experience you gain from
conquering that fear is priceless. The feelings of butterflies in your stomach to that sick feeling. You may not have the shiny medal, but you get feedback from the judges as where you could improve and also you get the satisfaction of doing something that you were afraid to attempt.

Let's apply this to life, by conquering a fear you will be able to apply the same principle to many other things. If you never try then you will never know. It will always be a what if?

Now when you have an opportunity to conquer fear, make sure you face it head on and break the walls down.

Do something amazing and test yourself, you never know what the outcome might be.

*A wise Sensei once said
in a dojo not so far away*

"Mokuso"

Let's dig deeper into the why here guys and go down the rabbit hole. This is done twice in every class for a reason.
Once at the start and once at the end. At the start it is to help clear your mind from your day, to create space for everything you are about to learn.

It is done at the end of class as a form of reflection. It allows you to absorb
what you have learnt in class.

So now when you are next in class and Sensei calls "Mokuso" remember why we do it and use this to help focus your mind so that you can get the most out of your class.

*A wise Sensei once said
in a dojo not so far away*

"Anyone can punch or kick.
In the dojo you learn how not to punch or kick."

-Author Unknown

At first that seems like huh? Why do we train then? But if you look deeper into it and you will see "It's the art of fighting without fighting"- Bruce Lee.

Most martial artists are nice people. Look at the dojo you train in, most
people are nice (with the exception of your Sensei when he or she is angry).

Jokes aside in a dojo you learn how to control your emotions and avoid violence where possible and to use the skills you learn only when necessary.

*A wise Sensei once said
in a dojo not so far away*

**"Do not strike others and do not allow others to strike you.
The goal is peace without incident."**

- Chojun Miyagi

On the surface this sounds like a very passive, avoid violence type of quote. If you read into it more you will see that there is more to it.

This is basically promoting verbal de escalation In a situation to help diffuse it i.e. One of the greatest self defence tips avoidance.

However it does also say that you should defend yourself if someone is trying to strike you.

Remember even if you are a pacifist. The passive attitude should come from strength and confidence rather than fear. It's better to have the knowledge of how to defend yourself and no need to use it rather than being in a situation where you need to defend yourself and not having the ability to do so.

*A wise Sensei once said
in a dojo not so far away*

"Once a kata has been learned, it must be practised repeatedly until it can be applied in an emergency, for knowledge of just the sequence of a kata in karate is useless."

– Gichin Funakoshi

This is a great one from the founder of Shotokan Karate and also the person who is known as the fore father of modern karate. Let's apply this to
confrontation kata. It's good knowing the pattern and it looking pretty, but ask yourself will my kicks stop an attacker who is intent on knocking my head off?

If you concentrate purely on aesthetics over effectiveness then kata may aswell be a dance rather than a self defence 'map' as it should be.

Always look at the principles hidden in the kata not just the movements. This will help develop effectiveness and power in your technique.

This will allow you to apply these to other areas of your karate.
Just an example bursting, this teaches you the principle of moving into the eye of the storm and stopping a technique as early as possible.

This can also be applied to blocking round kicks with Oshikomu uke. You move into the kick and stop it as early as possible.

*A wise Sensei once said
in a dojo not so far away*

"The secret principle of martial arts is not vanquishing the attacker, but resolving to avoid an encounter before its occurrence. To become an object of an attack is an indication that there was an opening in one's guard, and the important thing is to be on guard at all times."

– *Gichin Funakoshi*

Looking at this quote, basically the traditional way to describe awareness or "zanshin".

Always be aware of your surroundings, as the old saying goes "prevention is
better than cure."

*A wise sensei once said
in a dojo not so far away*

"If you find yourself in a fair fight your tactics suck!"

-John Steinbeck

This one I will credit not to the Sensei that said it but to the original person to have said it, author John Steinbeck.

Breaking it down in a sparring bout or even self defence situation your aim is to gain an advantage over your opponent. So your tactics should reflect this ideology. Just an example if you are fighting someone stronger than yourself then you should ideally keep them away, as if they hit you it will hurt, alternatively they could possibly grab you with the view to either control or take you down. In this instance use your kicks to control the distance and gain the advantage. If you play the strength game in that situation you risk loosing or worse depending on the situation.

So the long and short of it guys fight smart not hard. Keep the tools that work for you and be familiar with the ones that don't work as well. Arm yourselves for success both inside and outside of the dojo.

*A wise Sensei once said
In a dojo not so far away*

"How do you eat an elephant?
One bite at a time."

Let's apply this principle to learning a new kata. You can try and run through the whole kata and you will eventually pick it up.

Why not break it down into sequences and learn those, then put it all together? This will allow you to learn it faster and also allow you to work on the individual techniques involved too.

So when you next go to learn a kata, remember break it down and digest it bit by bit.

Chapter 4

Determination & Spirit

*A wise Sensei once said
in a dojo not so far away*

"If you are walking through a forest and someone overtakes you. Does this change the scenery?"

Let's break this down in karate terms. We are all on a journey to achieve a goal. That goal is personal and individual to you all. How long it takes to get there doesn't matter as long as every step you take is one that pushes you towards the final destination.

If someone reaches that milestone faster than you then so what? Your journey to your goal is exactly that, yours. As long as you are taking positive measures to help you move forwards then why does it matter how long it takes?

*A wise Sensei once said
in a dojo not so far away*

"One whose spirit and mental strength have been strengthened by sparring with a never-say-die attitude should find no challenge too great to handle.
One who has undergone long years of physical pain and mental agony to learn one punch, one kick, should be able to face any task, no matter how difficult, and carry it through to the end.
A person like this can truly be said to have learned karate."

– *Gichin Funakoshi*

This is a great quote from the founder of modern karate. It basically shows how martial arts can build character and also how this can further be applied to modern life.

Lets take a grading as an example. You push your body beyond your limits all for the next grade a darker coloured belt. The satisfaction you receive from taking a beating and getting back up cannot be expressed in words. This teaches you to keep going even when your body says no more, you keep pushing as you want it that bad. If you can push yourself that far for a piece of cotton that holds your trousers up, then why can't you achieve other goals?

So the long and the short of this use what you learn in your martial arts training and apply it both inside and outside the dojo too.

*A wise Sensei once said
in a dojo not so far away*

"Focus on the end result you want. Not what may be happening at this moment."

-Jason Smith

Let's break this down a second. Focus and mindset play a big part in achieving any goal. There is an old saying "one tree can give a thousand match sticks, but it takes one match stick can burn down a whole forest". Think of negative thoughts as a match stick. It takes one negative thought to destroy that positive mindset.

Let's apply this to the dojo. You may have had a hard session where you are
trying to learn a new kata. If at the end of the session you think I will never get this, then guess what?

You have defeated yourself already. Instead try and think positive thoughts such as I may not have learnt the whole thing tonight, but at least I know the first three moves or whatever it may be.

So when you next finish a class at the dojo look at the positives from that session and look for ways to improve and grow. Try not to dwell on the negatives as this will hinder your progress and stump your growth.

Remember train hard and be awesome.

*A wise Sensei once said
in a dojo not so far away*

"You must understand that there is more than one path to the top of the mountain."

-Miyamoto Musashi

Let's break this down. You may be climbing a mountain and reaching the peak may be your goal. If you encounter an obstacle on that path say a fallen tree and you can't get through, you always have routes around it rather than having to turn back and give up. Always look for a way to move forwards and keep your eye on the end prize.

Applying this to karate, lets say you are practicing a kata that involves a jump such as Empi. If you have weak knees or are unable to jump. You can still perform the jump as more of a turn rather than a jump with strong form and kamae. This will allow you to perform the kata taking into account your limitations.

Keep positive and train hard.

A wise Sensei once said in a dojo not so far away

"Fall down 7 times get up 8"

-Famous Japanese Proverb

Always be determined to achieve your goals. No matter what obstacles you may face, determination will help you overcome them.

Do not give up on your dreams as with the right planning and actions you can make what seems impossible, possible.

Never give up and always be positive.

*A wise Sensei once said
in a dojo not so far away*

"Quitters never win
and
winners never quit."

Let's break this down. If you quit at the sign of adversity then guess what? You loose the battle and you will nearly always look for the easy routes through life. If you dust yourself off and persevere you will not only grow, but you will also become a stronger individual.

So let's build that strength and keep on pushing. No matter what obstacles you may face, there is always a way through. Just keep moving forward and remain positive.

*A wise Sensei once said
in a dojo not so far away*

"The enemy may break your bones, but do not let them break your spirit."

As long as you believe in yourself you can achieve anything as soon as you give up on yourself you have lost the battle and your opponent has won.

Bones will heal, but loss of spirit in a self defence situation can be dire.
So stay strong and keep believing.

*A wise Sensei once said
in a dojo not so far away*

"Train like a black belt"

-Kirsty Mallinder

This one speaks for itself to be fair. As the old saying goes "a black belt doesn't give you magical super powers. It's the years of preparation for that moment that give you those abilities." So if you think I will try hard when I get there, to be honest and blunt you won't ever reach that milestone. You need to adapt the mindset of good training values to ensure when you do get there it is habit already.

Remember a black belt is the same as a white belt, except it's darker. In all
seriousness it's a great achievement, but the preparation is what makes the achievement all that bit sweeter. "The more sugar you put in the sweeter the
batter."

Now when you are next in a dojo remember to "train like a black belt".

*A wise Sensei once said
in a dojo not so far away*

"Keep up the positive attitude it will take you far"

- Mr JP

This has to be credited to the person who originally said this, known as Mr JP.

By focusing your energy on positive actions that will help you to improve such as pushing down in your stances or relaxing during kata to increase speed.

Negativity destroys morale and gives bad results.

So when you next finish class look at the positive things that you have achieved, so maybe you learnt a new technique or you nailed a kata. Whatever it may be, ensure you focus on the positives to help you to grow.

Printed in Great Britain
by Amazon